W9-AAT-586

MAKE ME THE BEST

LACROSSE PLAYER

BY JESS MYERS

SportsZone

An Imprint of Abdo Publishing
abdopublishing.com

abdopublishing.com

Published by Abdo Publishing, a division of ABDO, PO Box 398166, Minneapolis, Minnesota 55439. Copyright © 2017 by Abdo Consulting Group, Inc. International copyrights reserved in all countries. No part of this book may be reproduced in any form without written permission from the publisher. SportsZone™ is a trademark and logo of Abdo Publishing.

Printed in the United States of America, North Mankato, Minnesota
102016
012017

Cover Photos: Peter Dean/Shutterstock Images, top left; CLS Digital Arts/Shutterstock Images, top right; James A. Boardman/Shutterstock Images, middle left; Catwalk Photos/Shutterstock Images, bottom left; Geoff Robins/Canadian Press/AP Images, bottom right
Interior Photos: Peter Dean/Shutterstock Images, 4 (top); James A. Boardman/Shutterstock Images, 4 (middle); Catwalk Photos/Shutterstock Images, 4 (bottom); CLS Digital Arts/Shutterstock Images, 4–5 (top); Geoff Robins/Canadian Press/AP Images, 4–5 (bottom); Brian A. Westerholt/Getty Images Sport/Getty Images, 7; Jamie Sabau/Getty Images Sport/Getty Images, 8; Jim Rogash/Getty Images Sport/Getty Images, 11; Justin Edmonds/Getty Images Sport/Getty Images, 13; Marc Piscotty/Getty Images Sport/Getty Images, 15; Rick Stewart/Getty Images Sport/Getty Images, 16–17; Jack Dempsey/Getty Images Sport/Getty Images, 18–19; Scott Bales/YCJ/Icon Sportswire, 21; Alex Cena/ZumaPress/Newscom, 23, 24–25; Nick Wass/AP Images, 27; Ricky Carioti/The Washington Post/Getty Images, 29; Peyton Williams/Getty Images Sport/Getty Images, 30–31; Lance King/Getty Images Sport/Getty Images, 32–33; Rich Barnes/Icon Sportswire, 35; Drew Hallowell/Getty Images Sport/Getty Images, 37; Icon SMI 766/Icon SMI/Newscom, 39; Jerome Davis/Icon SMI/Newscom, 40–41; Mike Ridewood/Icon Sportswire, 43; Rich Barnes/Cal Sport Media/Newscom, 45

Editor: Patrick Donnelly
Series Designer: Nikki Farinella
Content Consultant: Chip Rogers, Former Chair, US National Women's Lacrosse Team Committee

Publisher's Cataloging-in-Publication Data

Names: Myers, Jess, author.
Title: Make me the best lacrosse player / by Jess Myers.
Description: Minneapolis, MN : Abdo Publishing, 2017. | Series: Make me the best athlete | Includes bibliographical references and index.
Identifiers: LCCN 2016945674 | ISBN 9781680784909 (lib. bdg.) | ISBN 9781680798180 (ebook)
Subjects: LCSH: Lacrosse--Juvenile literature.
Classification: DDC 796.34--dc23
LC record available at http://lccn.loc.gov/2016945674

TABLE OF

CONTENTS

INTRODUCTION

Modern lacrosse games look very different from the sport's early days. Lacrosse developed hundreds of years ago among native people in what is now the eastern United States and Canada. Today the game still combines speed, skill, strategy, and physical play. That hasn't changed a bit.

Lacrosse is a sport of talented scorers, such as Canadian legend Gary Gait. Goaltenders like Liz Hogan and defenders like Sloane Serpe try to keep opposing teams in check. Passing and catching are the most basic skills in the game. Few are better at them than Will Manny. And players like Anthony Kelly and Kayla Treanor are masters at winning draws and faceoffs.

At one point, all of these stars were young boys and girls with lacrosse sticks and dreams of being the best. Thanks to hard work and good coaching, they found success at the college, professional, and international levels. And they achieved their dreams of being the best lacrosse players in the world.

PASS AND CATCH LIKE

WILL MANNY

Passing and catching the ball are among the first skills that young lacrosse players should learn. They're also the most important skills to practice while learning the game. Strong passing and catching is the quickest way to move from one end of the field to the other. It's also the key to scoring goals and intercepting passes intended for an opponent.

Manny tells young players that it's important to get used to the feel of a lacrosse stick in their hands, even if they just toss and catch a ball while sitting on the couch.

Will Manny is a star forward in Major League Lacrosse (MLL), the top outdoor lacrosse league in the United States. He played college lacrosse for the University of Massachusetts (UMass), one of the top college programs in the nation.

Will Manny looks to pass to an open teammate.

Manny was a first-team All-America pick at UMass. In 2012 he was a finalist for the Tewaaraton Award, which is given to the top college lacrosse player in the country. After college Manny was an assistant coach at Wagner University for two years. In 2016 he joined the staff at the University of Utah.

After graduating from college with an economics degree, Manny's first job was working for a bank in Boston. He left the position after a time to coach lacrosse instead.

PASS LIKE WILL MANNY

- Remember the "Four Ps" to become a better passer and catcher.

- PUSH your top hand toward your target as you PULL the butt end of your stick with your bottom hand. That action creates a push-pull motion.

- POINT the head of your stick at your target after you push and pull and the ball is about to release out of your stick. Pointing helps you know where the ball is going.

- Finally, you want your bottom hand to finish in your hip POCKET. That means you followed through with your hands.

A strong top hand helps Manny direct his passes.

Like most lacrosse players, Manny makes his mark by passing and catching. He is known as an incredible goal scorer. But Manny is more focused on getting passes to teammates and putting them in positions to score. That is the essence of a sport based on teamwork.

Manny stands 5 feet 9 inches (175 cm) tall. He weighs 160 pounds (73 kg). That means he's usually one of the smallest players on the field. Smaller players can make up for their lack of size by perfecting stick skills, such

HANNAH NIELSEN

Hannah Nielsen is from Australia. Christmas comes in the summer for Aussies. Maybe that warm-weather season of giving helped Nielsen learn that it's better to give than to receive. Nielsen played four seasons of college lacrosse at Northwestern University in Evanston, Illinois, where she became the most accomplished passer in the game. The Wildcats were 85–3 during her career there. They won four national titles in the process. And Nielsen was named the nation's top player twice. By the end of her college career, Nielsen held college records for most assists in a game, a season, and a career.

Manny works to get open when he doesn't have the ball.

When he is not playing or coaching, Manny helps run a lacrosse program to teach young players the game. as passing and catching. And the players with the best stick skills are the ones who usually get the most playing time.

One characteristic that makes Manny successful is that he has what he calls "soft hands." When you're catching, if you stab at the ball, you will have trouble controlling it. You have to let the ball come to you and receive it gently. Manny coaches players to think of the ball as an egg that they have to catch without breaking.

DRILL DOWN!

This three-person drill improves passing and catching skills.

1. Set two cones 10 yards apart with a player at each.

2. A third player runs at one cone, catching and returning a pass on the run.

3. When the player in the middle reaches the cone, he or she repeats the process in the opposite direction.

4. Continue for 60 seconds, switching hands and shoulders often. Then repeat with a different player in the middle.

WIN FACEOFFS LIKE
ANTHONY KELLY

To win a lacrosse game, your team needs to score goals. To score goals, you need to possess the ball. A good way for your team to get the ball is to have a talented faceoff person. That's why several lacrosse teams have been happy to have Anthony Kelly wear their colors.

As a faceoff specialist, Kelly often breaks the head of his stick. He once broke four heads in a game. He sometimes takes six sticks to the field for games.

Some players carry a lacrosse stick before they can even walk. But Kelly didn't start playing the game until he was in high school in northern Ohio. His favorite game had been ice hockey when he was younger. Despite his late start in lacrosse, he quickly caught up with his more experienced teammates and opponents.

Anthony Kelly, *top*, leans on an opponent to win a faceoff.

14

Part of Kelly's quick success came from his internal drive. As someone who admits he's always been stubborn, Kelly loves the one-on-one aspect of a faceoff. Within the boundaries of a team sport, Kelly found his calling at the middle of the field.

WIN FACEOFFS LIKE ANTHONY KELLY

- Develop quick hands by practicing faceoffs without a stick, using just your hands.

- Find your own style that is comfortable and successful for you. Some people prefer going down on one knee, some go on two knees, and some crouch.

- Listen for the whistle. Train your body to move as soon as the whistle is blown. Some faceoff specialists listen to whistles blown at random on their headphones. It gets them used to moving at the first sound.

- Have a plan for success. Know where your teammates are going to be when the whistle blows. Try to direct the ball to one of them to start an offensive possession.

Kelly, *right*, wins a faceoff against Greg Gurenlian.

Faceoffs occur at the start of each half and after every goal. In the men's game, the referee places a ball at the center of the field. Then one player from each team puts his stick next to the ball. (In women's lacrosse, faceoffs are called *draws*. See more details at the end of this chapter.) When the referee blows the whistle, the players fight to gain possession for their team. Often both players get to the ball at the same time. The stronger and more aggressive player usually wins that battle.

GREG GURENLIAN

Faceoff specialists often are referred to as "FOGO" players. That's short for "faceoff, get off." That means they take a faceoff, then get off the field and are replaced by another player until the next faceoff. Former Penn State star Greg Gurenlian said he's changing "FOGO" to "FoSho." That's short for "faceoff, shoot." Gurenlian has earned a reputation as a successful and intimidating faceoff man in MLL play. But with a hulking frame and the ability to shoot and score in bunches, he's known as a scorer, too. That makes him a threat for opponents and a fan favorite.

Kelly muscles his way to another faceoff win.

Kelly says there is no secret to his success. He wins faceoffs by working hard and practicing constantly. Kelly studies the techniques of other faceoff specialists who were successful in the past. He knows you're never too old to learn a trick or two that might help sharpen your skills. It's made him one of the most successful faceoff specialists of all time.

Syracuse senior Kayla Treanor led the nation with 217 draws controlled in 2016.

In the women's game, the play starts with a draw rather than a faceoff. In a draw, two opponents hold their sticks waist-high and the umpire places the ball between their pockets. When the umpire blows the whistle, the person with the quickest hands has the advantage.

Position yourself in a strong, athletic stance, allowing you to use your legs and core to help you control the ball. If you can get the ball on the back of your stick, you can fling it up or over your shoulder to a teammate. You can also try to push it forward to start a fast break.

DRILL DOWN!

Work on controlling where the ball goes after you win a faceoff.

1. Line up for a mock faceoff with the ball on the ground. A teammate or coach should stand nearby with a whistle.

2. When the whistle is blown, clamp your stick on the ball as quickly as possible. Pull the ball backward between your legs and pass to a teammate. Repeat five times.

3. Next, when the whistle is blown, clamp your stick on the ball and push it forward, past the opposing faceoff person, to start a fast break. Repeat five times.

PLAY GOALTENDER LIKE

LIZ HOGAN

Some players say the greatest feeling in the game comes from scoring a goal. But Liz Hogan says she gets a bigger thrill from preventing the ball from going into the net.

Hogan is a goaltender. It's a tough job, both physically and mentally. Lacrosse balls are hard, and getting hit with them can hurt. And there's so much pressure on the goaltender to work with her defenders and keep the opponent from scoring.

Hogan and her twin sister, Allyson, have played lacrosse together since second grade. Allyson is an attacker, so Liz would often train by trying to stop her sister's shots.

Hogan started playing lacrosse in second grade in her hometown in western New York. The community didn't have a girls' team. So Liz and

Liz Hogan keeps her eye on the ball wherever it is—even when it's behind the net.

her twin sister, Allyson, played on boys' teams until sixth grade. Playing with boys got them used to a faster version of the game.

Goaltenders have many responsibilities. They have to direct the defense and clear the ball out of the zone

PLAY GOALTENDER LIKE LIZ HOGAN

- Get the best equipment possible. Your helmet is especially important, because it protects you against concussions.

- Know where the ball is at all times. Shots can come at you from any angle and from anywhere on the field.

- Work on passing and ground balls with the rest of the team. Your stick skills need to be strong, especially when clearing the ball.

- Watch the shooters' eyes. They're usually focused on their target.

- Step to the shooter to cut down the angle. Attack a bounce shot—smother it if you can, rather than letting it bounce at you.

- Remember to communicate with your teammates. You're the only person who can see what is happening on the field at all times. Take charge and be loud!

Hogan is a take-charge player who calls out directions to her teammates.

When she played softball as a girl, Liz was a catcher. By the time she made the transition back to lacrosse, she was used to catching and blocking balls.

after making a save. But their most important job is keeping the ball out of the net. It helps that goalies are the only players with full access to the goal crease or circle. That's a ring around the net that attacking players cannot enter.

Hogan starred at Syracuse University from 2007 to 2011. Since then she has been an assistant coach at Colgate,

JESSE SCHWARTZMAN

During his years of playing college and professional lacrosse, Jesse Schwartzman earned the nickname "Bear." But based on his performance in goal, "Mr. Perfect" might have been a more appropriate nickname. At Johns Hopkins University in Maryland, Jesse led the Blue Jays to a perfect 16–0 record and the national title in 2005. He did it again with the MLL's Denver Outlaws in 2013. Schwartzman was the league's top goalie as the Outlaws became the MLL's first team to record a perfect regular season, going 14–0. Schwartzman set the league record for the best goals-against average that year.

Jesse Schwartzman makes a big save for Johns Hopkins in a game against Duke.

Virginia Tech, and Stanford. She also was chosen to play for the US women's national team in 2015. And she was a charter member of the first women's professional league, which started in 2016.

Hogan was the fourth overall pick in the 2016 United Women's Lacrosse League draft. She was chosen by the Boston Storm, one of four teams in the league.

Hogan is also helping teach the next generation of lacrosse stars. She started her own company that focuses on developing players. She says she finds great satisfaction in working with young players, assisting in their physical and mental development, and helping them reach their goals. It's an interesting turn of events for somebody who has dedicated her career to preventing others from scoring goals.

DRILL DOWN!

Use tennis balls in this drill to warm up before practice or games.

1. With a goaltender in the net, Players A and B stand side by side in front of the net. Player A has a stick. Player B has a bag of tennis balls.

2. Player B quickly feeds tennis balls to Player A, who shoots at the goalie as soon as a ball is in her mesh.

3. The shooter should fire both high and low shots and work on getting the goalie moving from side to side.

PLAY DEFENSE LIKE

SLOANE SERPE

In men's lacrosse, defenders stay on their side of the field. In women's lacrosse, defenders go all over the place. In both games, defenders support the goaltender by keeping opponents from getting an easy route to the net. They often control the pace of the game. And they make sure the opposing attackers never get too comfortable.

Shannon Smith was a dominant attacker for Northwestern. Serpe was an elite defender at North Carolina. The two were archrivals in college. Later they became friends and teammates with Team USA.

Sloane Serpe enjoys frustrating and disrupting the opponent. She was a multisport athlete growing up in New Jersey. Sloane was aggressive in sports such as lacrosse and ice hockey, where she played almost exclusively on boys' teams.

Sloane Serpe, *right*, works hard to keep up with a Northwestern attacker.

She usually played midfield in high school. But when recruiters from the University of North Carolina came calling, they asked her to play defense.

Serpe's aggressive nature served her well as a college player. She quickly learned that making a good play on defense translates into immediate offense for her team.

PLAY DEFENSE LIKE SLOANE SERPE

- Use your stick and your body to prevent your opponent from having a clear look at your net or a clear route to get there.

- Pay attention to your footwork. Your feet put you into position to defend. Quickness and agility are important.

- Also watch your body positioning. In a strong defensive stance, you want your arms out, your hips down, and your back arched.

- Make sure your legs, ankles, and feet are loose and warmed up before practices and games.

- Be aggressive. Don't sit back and wait for the player with the ball to make a move. Instead, play fast and make the player with the ball keep guessing where you're going to go.

Serpe, *left*, gets physical with attackers when necessary.

As a senior at North Carolina, Serpe had 40 ground balls and caused 19 turnovers. She was nominated for the Tewaaraton Award.

As a freshman, she joined a team with three seniors on defense and learned the ropes from them immediately. A year later, with those seniors gone, Serpe took on a leadership role with the Tar Heels. She mentored younger players and helped North Carolina win the national title in 2013, during her junior year.

Serpe got used to matching up against one of the opponent's best offensive players. She found she loved

TUCKER DURKIN

Florida's MLL team is called the Launch, in honor of the state's history of launching spacecraft. It's an appropriate place for Tucker Durkin to play. He's long been known for using his size and skill to launch attackers off their feet when they make a move toward his net. Durkin was named the top defender in the country as a senior at Johns Hopkins. He was the third overall pick in the MLL draft in 2013. After beginning his professional career in Canada, Durkin came to Florida in 2014. He quickly became a fan favorite for his big hits and intense play.

Tucker Durkin, *right*, knocks the ball away from a North Carolina attacker.

the individual battles, trying to force a foe to make a mistake. Her leadership and on-field success didn't go unnoticed. Serpe was a three-time All-American and finished her career as the university's all-time leader in games started.

In 2015 Serpe was hired as an assistant coach at Yale University. She's also a member of the US women's national team. Serpe still focuses on working with defensive teammates to force the opponent to abandon their offensive plans or turn the ball over, allowing the defense to turn the play in the other direction. That's the key to successful defense, and the part of the game that players like Serpe do best.

In addition to lacrosse, Serpe loved to play hockey as a teenager. She usually played on boys' teams, and she said that her naturally aggressive play led to many penalties.

DRILL DOWN!

The "Tap-Tap" drill helps develop defensive footwork.

1. One coach stands in front of one to eight players, spread out with three to five yards between them.

2. When the coach moves her hand, the players move in that direction. The coach says "tap-tap" each time so the players get used to audible clues as well.

3. The coach should direct the players randomly in all four directions. Players maintain proper body position as they move.

4. Do the drill for a minute, allow a rest, and then repeat.

SHOOT AND SCORE LIKE

GARY GAIT

Many skills and many players are involved in winning a lacrosse game. But the ability to shoot and score often has the biggest impact on a team winning a game. Few players have ever done that more often or more creatively than the talented Canadian Gary Gait.

Gait and his wife, Nicole, have two children. Their daughter, Taylor, played midfield for her father at Syracuse. Their son, Braedon, played midfield at Princeton University.

Gait and his twin brother, Paul, played four seasons at Syracuse University starting in 1987. They led the Orange to three national championships. And Gary's ability to score goals like nobody had seen before was a big part of that success.

Gary Gait prepares to shoot in an indoor lacrosse game.

Shooting and scoring involves using your arms and leverage to fling the ball from the head of the stick toward the net. Shooting is one of the first skills young players learn after passing and catching. As players get older and stronger, the speed of the ball increases. The best players in the world have been known to shoot lacrosse balls at

SHOOT AND SCORE LIKE GARY GAIT

- Be creative. If your opponent is studying you, they will learn your favorite route to the net. When they think they have you figured out, do something they don't expect.

- Switch things up when shooting. The goaltender has a lot of net to cover. Aim for the corners, both upper and lower. That will keep the goalie guessing.

- Have patience. Don't be afraid to wait if there's not an obvious opening. Work for a better shot or pass to an open teammate.

- Work on your shot constantly. The best players have been known to spend hours shooting at a wall and catching the rebound. Regular, intense practice will help develop your speed and accuracy.

Gait fought through constant defensive pressure to become one of the greatest scorers ever.

speeds faster than 100 miles per hour (161 km/h). That's tough enough for a goaltender to see, let alone stop.

And try as they might over the course of Gait's 17 professional seasons, opponents rarely found a way to stop him. His prolific scoring helped his teams win many titles. In addition to that trio of national titles in college, Gait helped his team win three indoor pro lacrosse titles. He also won three outdoor pro lacrosse titles, three senior

▌IIIIIIII Paul Rabil's wife, Kelly, is a member of the US women's national team and won a World Cup in 2013.

PAUL RABIL

From his hometown in Maryland, Paul Rabil didn't travel far to play college lacrosse. He starred at Johns Hopkins and has continued to shine in MLL. Rabil was the first pick in the 2008 draft. Playing for the Boston Cannons and New York Lizards has helped the two-time MLL Most Valuable Player keep a high profile. Rabil has earned endorsement deals for energy drinks and equipment that have made him one of the most popular and well-known names in the sport.

Gait waves to the crowd at his last National Lacrosse League all-star game appearance in 2005.

men's lacrosse titles in Canada, and world championships in both indoor and outdoor lacrosse.

Gait began coaching while still playing professionally. He worked as an assistant at the University of Maryland. He helped the women's team there win seven national titles. In 2007 he returned to Syracuse as the head coach of its women's team.

While playing professional indoor lacrosse, Gait led the league in scoring seven times. He retired in 2005 as the league's all-time leading scorer with 1,091 career points.

Scoring a goal is one of the most exciting plays in lacrosse. And in the history of the game, hardly anyone has done it like Gary Gait.

DRILL DOWN!

The Mirror Drill emphasizes teamwork and finishes with a shot on the net.

1. Player A runs back and forth behind the net with the ball. Players B and C mirror his actions 10 yards in front of the net, 10 yards apart.

2. On the coach's whistle, Player A passes to Player B, who in turn passes to Player C. He can either pass it back or shoot.

3. Add defenders and a goalie to make the passing and shooting more challenging.

GLOSSARY

ASSIST

A pass that leads to a goal for a teammate.

ATTACKER

Also called a forward, the player usually located in a team's offensive end trying to score goals.

CREASE

A circle around the net in which no attacking players are allowed to set foot.

FACEOFF

A battle for possession of the ball between two opponents inside the center circle.

HEAD

The end of the lacrosse stick where the ball is carried in a mesh pocket.

MESH

An interlaced structure often made from cloth or wire threads; the pocket of a lacrosse stick is made from mesh.

SAVE

When a goaltender blocks the ball from going in the net.

FOR MORE INFORMATION

BOOKS

Bowker, Paul. *Total Lacrosse*. Minneapolis, MN: Abdo Publishing, 2017.

Coulson, Art. *The Creator's Game: A Story of Baaga'adowe/ Lacrosse*. St. Paul, MN: Minnesota Historical Society Press, 2013.

Rogers, Kate. *Girls Play Lacrosse*. New York: PowerKids Press, 2016.

WEBSITES

To learn more about lacrosse, visit **booklinks.abdopublishing.com**. These links are routinely monitored and updated to provide the most current information available.

PLACE TO VISIT

National Lacrosse Hall of Fame and Museum
2 Loveton Circle
Sparks, Maryland, 21152
(410) 235-6882
www.uslacrosse.org/about-us-lacrosse/museum
Lacrosse fans can discover and relive the origins of the game through rare photographs and art, vintage equipment and uniforms, sculptures and trophies, and other memorabilia and artifacts. The game's all-time greats are honored in the Hall of Fame Gallery.

INDEX

ABOUT THE AUTHOR

Jess Myers attended his first college lacrosse game in the spring of 2000—Princeton at Brown—and was hooked immediately. He raised two lacrosse-playing sons and enjoys few things more than a sunny afternoon at a field watching the game. This is his third children's book. He also writes about hockey, basketball, football, travel, politics, and the outdoors. Myers lives near St. Paul, Minnesota, with his wife and three children.